The Legacy Builder

Forming Habits to Live a Life of Significance

Rosemary Margaret Ford

Table of Contents

The greatest glory in living lies not in never falling, but in rising every time we fall.

Chapter 1. Introduction

Step into the world of greatness through our Special Report: "The Legacy Builder: Forming Habits to Live a Life of Significance". This enlightening journey isn't about merely passing your days, it's about creating a life that outlasts you, a legacy endowed with purpose and meaning. Benefit from years of research, heartening stories, and practical, easy-to-follow steps that unlock the immense potential within you to achieve real life successes. Filled to the brim with exciting revelations and presented in a friendly, engaging manner, this report stands as your blueprint to leaving your indelible mark on the world. So why wait? Grab your copy today and embark on the rewarding journey to becoming a builder of a truly meaningful and impactful legacy!

Chapter 2. Introduction: The Pursuit of Significance

From the dawn of civilization, humanity has been defined by an unquenchable yearning. A ceaseless quest for significance that transcends the confines of a mere physical existence, venturing into the spiritually and emotionally profound. This insatiable thirst for meaning is a universal, fundamentally human experience. It drives us to seek something greater than ourselves, a higher purpose that can give our ephemeral lives a lasting impact. A legacy.

2.1. Understanding Our Craving for Significance

The desire for significance, for leaving a lasting impact on the world, is a deep-seated need that pervades all human lives. This need is often conflated with the desire for fame or success, yet it's important to distinguish between them. Fame and success, while tangible and easily measurable, provide only temporary satisfaction. True significance, on the other hand, is derived from positively impacting others' lives, creating something enduring, and forging a legacy that continues to inspire long after we're gone. It resides in the realm of the enduring, the timeless, the boundlessly meaningful.

We yearn to live lives marked by purpose and meaning—an ambition frequently hemmed in by the relentless march of time and the pressure of manifold, often trivial, daily pursuits. However, by harnessing the formidable power of habits and laser-focused goal-setting, we can ultimately direct our energies towards building a legacy that stands the test of time.

2.2. The Journey Towards Meaning

The pursuit of significance is a journey that invites us to gaze inward, reflecting deeply on our values, aspirations, and passions. It is a voyage of discovery enabling us to look beyond the superficial glare of worldly success and peer into what genuinely resonates with our core being, what actually matters.

As we embark on this quest, we will confront questions that challenge and provoke us—What mark will we leave on the world? What do we desire to be remembered for? These are not questions with straightforward answers. They require us to delve deep into our thoughts, beliefs, and life experiences. More importantly, they will inspire us to break free from the shackles of mindless routine and rigorously pursue a life of genuine significance.

2.3. The Power and Potential of Legacy-Focused Living

Embarking on the pursuit of significance by focusing on legacy offers immense advantages. Primarily, it directs our efforts towards the long-term, discouraging immediate gratification in favor of lasting impact. Moreover, owing to its expansive scope, it inspires us to think big—to transcend our personal needs and contribute to the welfare of the larger community. It broadens our perspectives, nudging us towards a path of selflessness and service to others.

Influencing another life positively, inspiring change, seeding an idea that grows and flourishes, building institutions that endure—the power and potential of these endeavors are limitless. Such legacy-oriented living fuels the heart with an undeniable sense of purpose, grounding us in a profound sense of fulfillment that evanescent flashes of personal success or wealth can never furnish.

2.4. Embracing the Challenge

In understanding this pursuit of significance, our endeavor is not without its challenges. Creating lasting change requires constant commitment, unremitting efforts, and a resolve to overcome obstacles in our path. It demands the courage to challenge the status quo, embrace vulnerability, and take decisive steps, despite uncertainties and risks.

However, the rewards of this pursuit are multiple and evergreen. Each of us holds the potential to create something meaningful, something that will endure and inspire others - a legacy that echoes through the corridors of time. By embracing the challenge, you enter into a process of personal transformation, thereby adding another layer of depth to your own experience of life.

In charting our course within this broad canvas, we'll move towards discussing an oft-neglected yet crucial aspect of our lives—the role of habits. Habits are the building blocks of our daily existence, influencing everything we do. As we progress through the forthcoming chapters, we'll uncover how these seemingly insignificant routines can empower us to build the life of significance we yearn for.

Together, we'll navigate through the unspoiled territories of habit formation, goal setting, resilience, social impact, and more. Each step, each page turned, brings us one step closer to understanding and embodying the legacy builder in every one of us, and forms a critical part of our collective journey towards a life of authentic significance.

Remember, the journey towards greatness doesn't come from fleeting achievements or momentary splendors. It resides within the passion-infused grind of our daily lives, in the unseen corners of our relentless pursuit of bettering ourselves and the world around us. It resides within every single choice we make impeccably until they cement into sturdy habits, cascading into a life truly worth living, a legacy worth leaving behind.

This desire for significance is not an idle daydream. It is a call to action, an invitation to step into your power and potential, and a challenge to live a life of intentionality, purpose, and profound impact. The quest has begun—let's step boldly into the world of greatness together.

Chapter 3. Understanding Legacy: More Than Just Wealth

Every generational cycle is beset with a daunting array of interpretations concerning the notion of legacy. Unfortunately, it is quite common for the concept to be stripped down to its most simplistic, materialistic construct - wealth. Examining it as something tangible and quantifiable, bound by financial competence and property ownership, restricts our realization of the broader and arguably more significant aspect of legacy. Placing wealth as the sole constitutive factor diminishes the impactful influence and resonance a true legacy can impart in our lives and those of the succeeding generations. Thus begins our journey into understanding legacy, not as mere wealth but as a beacon that illuminates and inspires the path of others.

3.1. Placing Wealth Into Perspective

Contrary to what many might believe, the legacy we leave behind does not orbit solely around financial affluence and amassed riches. Yes, money can help create opportunities and afford us a certain quality and comfort in life, but its importance reduces when it comes to preserving a legacy that endures throughout ages. The prominence of wealth should be weighed against what we, as legacy bearers, really want to communicate and pass on to future inheritors. Are we going to be remembered merely as the ones who left a hefty bank balance or as individuals that published an influential chapter in the book of life and society, thereby imprinting an indelible mark on the pages of history?

3.2. The Fabric of Legacy: Values, Wisdom, and Love

The texture of legacy is woven meticulously with the threads of values, wisdom, and love. Wealth is incapable of buying these virtues. Transmitting life experiences, sharing triumphs and failures, offering wisdom gleaned from an existence courageously lived, these form the true ethos of a profound legacy. Nurturing and instilling values in the younger generation, emphasizing the power of love, and encouraging tolerance and empathy narrates a story of a richer, celebrated life lived. This narrative, in the long run, illustrates a lasting legacy that resonates on a deeper, more personal level with those meant to inherit it.

3.3. Enduring Symbols and Their Influence

In the realm of heirlooms, those that carry a sense of purpose, affection, and historical links often stand out. They are the physical translators of one's legacy, embodying years of stories, experiences, and lessons that far outweigh their monetary worth. An old watch, a handwritten letter, a family photograph, they carry within themselves a nostalgia and sentiment that no amount of money can duplicate. They become symbols that serve to remind future generations of their roots, their heritage, and their responsibility to carry forth the legacy that has been passed onto them.

3.4. Contributions to the Greater Good

One of the most rewarding aspects of legacy is the impact one can make on the larger world. Going beyond monetary contributions, our ability to forsake immediacy for longevity and selfishness for selflessness underlines the potency of a strong legacy. Supporting institutions, communities, and causes beyond our lifetimes, devoting time and energy into molding something for the collective betterment, actively taking part in the society as responsible citizens – these components significantly influence how our legacy will shape up and be remembered.

In conclusion, while wealth does contribute to the security and ease of those who inherit our legacy, it is not the sole definer of it. A legacy run solely on the tracks of wealth misses the beautiful scenery around: of shared experiences, unique stories, imparted wisdom, and contributions to society. A legacy is a grand tapestry: every thread of experience, every color of emotion, every weave of wisdom makes it whole. Thus, it is pivotal to expand our comprehension of legacy beyond the simplistic confines of material wealth and embrace a more holistic understanding. This perspective readies us to start building not just a rich legacy but an equitable, profound and impactful one. In the subsequent chapters, we shall explore the various aspects of this truly meaningful construction.

Chapter 4. The Role of Habits: Shaping Our Future

Our journey commences with the understanding that the fabric of our lives is woven with the threads of habits. Weaving these threads consciously and judiciously lends the ultimate texture and contour to our life's tapestry, shaping it into a vibrant, purposeful, and enduring legacy. It's the sum total of these habits that define our actions, shape our destiny, and etch the signature of our legacy.

4.1. The Power of Habits

It's no secret that habits bear a remarkable impact on our lives. They structure our daily routine, influence our decisions, and shape our perceptions. Habits permeate every crevice of our existence so thoroughly that they often escape our conscious radar, working subtly and ceaselessly in the backdrop.

American philosopher William James beautifully encapsulated this sentiment when he said, "All our life, so far as it has definite form, is but a mass of habits."

But why do habits wield such immense power? The answer lies in the neurological phenomenon called 'Habit Loop'. This comprises three interconnected phases: the cue or trigger, the behaviour or routine, and the reward. The repetition of this loop fortifies the neural pathways linked to these habits, making them part of our unconscious reflexes. The more robust these paths, the more ingrained are our habits.

The power of habits is reflected not merely in the corpus of our daily actions, but also in the sequels that they engender. Our habits have the propensity to snowball into larger-scale life outcomes, both positive and negative. Consider the habits of regular exercise, reading, or meditating. The repeated and consistent practice of these forms an indomitable foundation of good health, knowledge, and mental equilibrium. Conversely, bad habits such as procrastination, unhealthy eating, or excessive worry can manifest into a shadow of poor health outcomes, lost opportunities and chronic stress.

4.2. The Nexus Between Habits and Legacy

The connection between habits and legacy is one that's intricate, consequential and far-reaching. Standing at this crossroad, it's essential to understand that every habit, no matter how minute, gradually paints the overarching picture of our legacy.

One may wonder how routine habits could potentially sculpt the monumental canvas of a legacy. The answer lies in the principle of aggregation of marginal gains, eloquently advocated by Sir Dave Brailsford, performance director of Team Sky, the British professional cycling team. The underlying essence of this principle is that small improvements or habits, when persistently practiced, sum up to significant transformations. This is rudimentarily analogous to how a succession of small rivulets converge into a majestic, life-sustaining river.

Here's another perspective: consider each habit as a brick. Some bricks may be robust, some might be frail; each one, however, contributes to form the ultimate structure of the edifice of your legacy. The selections of these bricks, their quality, and the care with which you lay them, contribute to the construction of your legacy. The resistance of this edifice against the rains of time and the winds of changes offers a testament to the strength of habits that constitute it.

4.3. Crafting Your Future with Good Habits

There's a universally acknowledged truth in the world of habit formation: good habits are hard to form but easy to live with, while bad habits are easy to form but hard to live with. The power to shape our future, therefore, somewhat lies in understanding this principle and using it to our advantage.

To create a life of purpose that transcends our earthly existence, weaving good habits into the fabric of our lives is essential. However, it is vital to remember that cultivating good habits isn't merely about sweeping, grand transformations; it's about the steady accumulation of tiny, sustainable changes. Engaging in simple practices such a gratitude journaling, exercising regularly, reading every day, practicing mindfulness can serve as foundation stones to accomplishing larger life goals. These habits don't just significantly enrich our personal lives, but also enable us to contribute effectively to the lives of others.

Remember, a journey of a thousand miles begins with a single step. Embark on this remarkable journey of shaping your future by conscientiously introducing, nurturing, and strengthening one good habit at a time.

4.4. Dismantling Destructive Habits

Just as constructing good habits is vital to building our legacy, breaking off the bonds of bad habits is equally crucial to hammering out a life of significance.

Unconstructive habits work insidiously, continuously chipping away at the magnificence we're meant to create. They are the unseen rogues that lurk in the shadows, gnawing at the roots of our potential.

To dismantle these, it's imperative to understand the mechanics of habit formation. Once the 'Habit Loop' is comprehended, we can interrupt this loop, replace the bad habits with good ones, and repeatedly reinforce these new behaviours until we rewire our neural pathways. This continuous cycle of Disrupt, Replace, Repeat forms the core strategy in breaking free from the shackles of destructive habits.

Remember, it's not storms, but the incessant trickling of water droplets that etches marks on the hardest of stones. So, depart from the path of intermittent grand resolutions, gravitate instead towards sustained and consistent efforts in breaking down destructive habits brick by brick.

Remember that our habits—good or bad—are our loyal servants. We build them first, and then, they build us. Crafting a life of significance, therefore, depends largely on the insights we garner about habit formation, and how skilfully we leverage them to weave the tapestry of our legacy.

Ultimately, we need to acknowledge the reality that our lives are bound by the threads of habits. How these threads are spun, dyed, and woven determines the intricate tapestry that is our legacy. It's time we take the reins of these habits in our own hands and shape them wisely to pursue a life of significance that leaves an enduring imprint on the sands of time.

Chapter 5. Identifying Life Goals: The Compass of Your Legacy

The essence of our unprecedented path to legacy building lies in the gravity of goals. Each goal, distinct and significant, then stitched capably into the rich tapestry of our lives, guides us like a compass towards the vision we hold for ourselves and the world we seek to influence. As the cornerstones of our pursuits, these objectives offer a paradigm through which we can not only understand our present actions but also forecast our future legacy.

5.1. Goals: The Foundation of Your Legacy

Begin to consider your life as a grand blueprint, every brick, every contour being a testament to your actions and attitudes. In this grand design, goals are the foundation. Strong, resilient, and well-articulated goals provide the base upon which you will erect your monumental legacy.

Understanding the importance of our ultimate objectives begins with introspection. Looking within ourselves, identifying our passions, strengths, aspirations, and challenges, acts as the necessary first step. It's the thrilling moment where we hold nothing back, exploring the terra incognita within us. This internal dialogue enables us to draft an illuminating list of possible objectives, marking the dawning steps in this journey.

5.2. Making Goals SMART

Ensure your goals are SMART - Specific, Measurable, Achievable, Relevant, and Time-bound. This powerful acronym lends tangible shape to your ambitions, allowing you to strategize efficiently. It's akin to sculpting clay into distinct forms, ensuring your ambition is purposefully directed, not squandered on vague aspirations.

+Specific: Address precisely what you aim to achieve, present it in clear, unequivocal terms that demystify your desire. +Measurable: Establish criteria to track your success with defined metrics for progress. +Achievable: Ensure the goal is realistic, considering the resources available and time required for completion. +Relevant: Solidify the connection between your goal and broader life vision, ensure it leaves a meaningful imprint on your legacy. +Time-bound: Implement a practical timeframe that creates a sense of urgency and subsequential dedication.

By doing so, you construct a pointed, substantial roadmap to achieving your future legacy.

5.3. Balancing Personal and Larger Goals

Legacy building is not exclusively about the large, grandiose goals we set for ourselves. It's an amalgamation of personal, professional, and philanthropic goals. Striking the right balance between these helps you live a more holistic life.

While personal and professional goals might be fulfilling on an individual level, incorporating philanthropic goals adds a larger dimension to your legacy building. We are, after all, social beings, and the connections we forge and the impact we make on the world carve out a considerable part of our legacy.

5.4. Embracing the Journey

Embrace the journey towards achieving your goals: the failures, the joy, the learnings, the uncertainty. Each represents unique brushstrokes of your legacy painting. Each failure becomes a lesson etched into your character's structure, while each success becomes a tale of triumph embedded in your life's narrative.

Understanding that goals are not merely endpoints but also processes catalyzes personal growth. And this very growth, this personal evolution, leads you to etch a deeper, more enriched legacy.

5.5. Review, Reflect, Revise

Like the seasons, our life circumstances and preferences evolve over time. Thus, incorporate a periodic review of your goals. Reflect on the efficacy of your strategies, recalibrate your compass, and if need be, redefine your goals to match your evolving desires.

This is not an admission of failure but an affirmation of growth, understanding that change is the only constant in life. Upholding adaptability categorically fosters your capability to build a notable legacy.

Through the identification and successful pursuit of life goals, you are the architect of your own existence, navigating the tumultuous seas of life resiliently, charting your course towards a meaningful legacy, grounded in purpose, enveloped in significance and eternally influential. Thus, your life goals become the compass of your legacy, guiding you towards charted territories of personal growth and meaningful contributions.

Chapter 6. Forming Good Habits: Small Steps to Big Changes

In this meaningful pursuit of legacy building, habits inevitably assume a gigantic role. The etching of these consistent practices into our daily life sketch a path leading us towards our desired legacy. Understandably, the phrase 'Forming Good Habits' may sound like an oversimplification. However, it's these seemingly minute steps that can lead to colossal transformations in our lives, settling indelibly within us and inevitably spurring bigger changes.

6.1. The Anatomy of a Habit

Let's dive into the intricate structure of a habit to understand its mechanics. A habit is primarily a three-part process that constitutes a loop: a cue that triggers the habit, the routine or behavior initiated by this cue, and finally, a reward that consolidates this system. Known as the Habit Loop, psychologist Charles Duhigg popularised this framework. It is critical to discern each part of your habit to alter or reinforce it.

The cue acts as a trigger or signpost indicating your brain to go into automatic mode. It can be a variety of inputs like time, location, feelings, or preceding events. The routine corresponds to the behavior, thought, or action that proceeds from this cue, and the reward is an incentive that satisfies a particular craving in your brain, fortifying the loop to repeat this habit in the future.

Understanding this structure can provide valuable insights during habit formation or modification. Only when we fully comprehend the workings of our habits can we successfully mould them according to our goals.

6.2. Habit Stacking: Building Upon Existing Habits

James Clear, the author of "Atomic Habits", introduces a strategy called 'Habit Stacking' which capitalises on the existing habits. It works by selecting a habit you perform consistently and appending a new behaviour to it.

To illustrate this concept, if you have a habit of having a cup of coffee in the morning, you can stack reading a book for 15 minutes onto it. Subsequently, this practice makes reading a part of your daily routine, forming a new positive habit. This connection between established and new behaviours can significantly smoothen the transition towards the inclusion of newer habits into your daily life.

6.3. Rewarding Yourself: The Power of Reinforcement

Positive reinforcement harbours immense potential to encourage habit formation. Rewards provide the brain with a sense of satisfaction and stimulate it to repeat the same behaviour to experience that pleasure again. It taps into the final section of the Habit Loop, solidifying the associations between the cue and the routine.

For instance, after a gruelling workout, having a refreshing protein smoothie can be an enticing reward. Over time, your brain starts associating the workout with the enjoyment derived from the smoothie, making it more likely that you will follow through with your exercise routine. It's important to remember that the reward should be beneficial and in alignment with your long-term goals.

6.4. Accountability Partner: The Power of Social Influence

Social accountability plays a significant role in shaping our habits. When we share our goals or new habits with someone we trust, we're more likely to follow through with them. An accountability partner can serve as a pillar of support during tough times, motivating us to persevere and providing feedback on our progress.

Seek out friends, family members, or mentors who can be a part of your habit-forming journey. These accountability partners add an exterior layer of responsibility and engagement, nudging us to roll out the actions towards achieving our goals, thereby enabling a robust habit-formation system.

6.5. Long-term Thinking: The Compound Effect

Often, the lack of immediate results can discourage us and derail our efforts in forming new habits. However, it's crucial to acknowledge that small steps stacked over time lead to significant changes, a pattern referred to as the Compound Effect. A 1% improvement each day might seem insignificant in the short term, but over the course of a year, it equals a 37% improvement.

Embracing a long-term perspective and remaining patient is integral to the process of good habit formation. Continuous small improvements can yield surprising results in the future, building a strong foundation for a significant legacy.

In conclusion, forming good habits is an incremental process that requires understanding the mechanics of habits, leveraging existing routines, incorporating positive reinforcement, building a social accountability system, and adopting a long-term perspective. Each of these small steps amalgamates to create a vigorous, vivacious path that facilitates the transformation of our everyday lives, enabling us to carve out lasting legacies. Embrace these techniques and chart your journey towards a fulfilling and meaningful life. The world awaits your legacy!

Chapter 7. Breaking Bad Habits: Disrupt, Replace, Repeat

In the compelling narrative that endeavors to etch out the road to a remarkable legacy, we now veer towards a critical juncture: breaking bad habits. This stride towards transformation involves three primary steps: disrupt, replace and repeat. Let's examine them in detail.

7.1. Disrupting the Routine

Making the conscious choice to break down the walls of your life's habits is the first, and arguably the most crucial step. These constructs, invisible yet significantly influential, give structure to our day. They determine our actions and reactions, often bypassing conscious thought. Therefore, the act of disrupting these 'autopilot modes' can be a significant challenge. To confront and acknowledge our bad habits is an act of courage that throws light on the darker corners of our existence. Self-awareness is a prerequisite to disruption. By identifying the triggers that commence these habits and the rewards they yield (whether they are emotional, physical, or mental), we break down the sequence that locks us in the cycle. The goal is not to criticize or judge oneself, but to understand what circumstances lead to automatic behaviors we would like to change.

7.2. Replacing with New, Constructive Alternatives

Once the disruptive process is successfully underway, the question that arises is what to do in the void that follows. It's essential to remember that the goal is not to eliminate old habits completely, but to replace them with new, healthier, more productive ones. The period post-disruption leaves room for change, a space that could just as quickly be filled again by destructive habits if left vacant. Therefore, it is beneficial to acknowledge the empty space and consciously fill it with new, healthier replacements.

To arrive at these new practices, we draw upon cognitive and behavioral science. Plunge into introspection and understand what you truly seek from your life. Engage with role models and mentors to gather inspiration and seek feasible replacements for your existing habits. Be realistic; select replacements that are achievable. The path towards change is often strewn with challenges; strive to steer clear of replacements that further complicate the route.

The replacements should not only be beneficial in themselves, but should also result in a meaningful or pleasurable outcome that will act as the reward to anchor the new habit. In context of a simple example, if you aim to replace a sedentary lifestyle with a more active one, the chosen physical activity itself should be enjoyable or the impact of a healthier, energized body a reward enough to keep you motivated.

7.3. The Cycle of Repetition: Cementing New Habits

The final step, repetition, is what cements the new habits in place, giving them the strength to resist the gravity that pulls us towards the familiarity and comfort of old habits. It is necessary to persist and repeat the newly adopted habit patterns for a definitive period until they get ingrained into our subconscious.

Scientific research sets a broad range of anywhere between 18 to 254 days to form a new habit, but patience is the touchstone of success here. Progress might be slow, and there will be days of setbacks, but maintaining a non-judgmental attitude towards oneself amidst this journey paves the way for persistence.

Bringing these three steps together, we discern a roadmap to initiate an empowering journey that breaks the shackles of bad habits and ushers in an era of change and growth. However, it's essential to note that the path to change is nonlinear and unique to each individual. Allow yourself to meander, to backtrack and realign your course. The process, although rigorous, is liberating in its outcome. It arms you with newfound strength, awareness, and resilience, establishing cornerstones for a legacy you'd wish to leave behind.

The voyage to build a legacy demands more than the breaking of bad habits. It seeks the forging of good ones, requests relationships, and resilience, and anticipates social impact, all of which form the subsequent chapters in this journey of significance.

Let's journey on. The road is long, but every step forward is a step towards greatness, towards a lasting, influential legacy. Let's disrupt, replace, and repeat, each part of this triad crucial as the wheels of meaningful change set in motion. These are the transformative understories of the legacy we are crafting, the tale of breaking bad habits —one disruption, one replacement, one repetition at a time. This is our legacy in the making, and indeed, there's no turning back now.

Thus, concludes the chapter dedicated to breaking bad habits, serving as an exhaustive guide to enable the reader to navigate through the intricate labyrinth of habits and construct a life pathway compatible with a legendary legacy. Tomorrow promises a new sunrise, with new habits, new relationships, and resilience in our quest to forge a significant legacy. Let's onward and ahead!

Chapter 8. Fostering Relationship: The Human Dimension of Legacy

In the realm of legacy building, fostering relationships assumes a central role, akin to the human heartbeat that keeps the construct of life pulsating with meaning and connection. This chapter delves into the intricate processes involved in nurturing these bonds, giving your legacy a human dimension that amplifies its significance.

8.1. The Value of Human Connection

At the core of our existence is an innate desire for connection, manifesting through our relationships with family, friends, and even with those who may merely pass through our lives. How we harness this intrinsic need to connect and nurture these relationships plays a crucial role in the creation of our legacy. Every interaction, every shared smile or tear, paves the way for a richer tapestry of interconnected significance.

In exploring the significance of human connection, we examine the roles of empathy and understanding, two elements that are fundamental to human communication. Empathy allows us to perceive and appropriately respond to the emotions of others, forming mindful connections. Understanding pertains to the cognitive aspect of communication, helping us navigate the complexities of human interaction and intentions.

8.2. Building Connections: A Stepwise Approach

Incorporating human connection into your legacy isn't something that occurs haphazardly. It requires a considered, methodical approach. This section lays out an easy-to-follow, step-by-step process, designed to enable you to construct meaningful relationships across various spheres of your life.

Step 1: Understanding Self: To foster meaningful connections, one must first comprehend their own identity, values, and expectations. This requires reflective practices such as journaling or contemplation, as tools for self-discovery.

Step 2: Embracing Differences: Each individual is unique, and recognizing these differences is key to avoiding misunderstandings and preserving relationships. Appreciate diversity and learn how to navigate through ideological disparities tactfully.

Step 3: Active Listening: Often, effective communication involves listening more and speaking less. Active listening not only means paying attention to words but also deciphering non-verbal cues, enhancing mutual understanding and respect.

Step 4: Sincere Communication: Authenticity forms the bedrock of enduring relationships. Whether it's expressing gratitude or articulating expectations, sincerity should always drive your interactions.

Step 5: Continuous Nourishment: Relationships are not static entities; they require constant care and attention. Regularly nourish your relationships by expressing appreciation, resolving conflicts promptly, and investing time and dedication into them.

8.3. The Influence of Relationships on Legacy

As we navigate through life, our relationships enrich our experiences and influence who we become, invariably shaping the legacy we leave behind. This section discusses the bi-directional link between relationships and legacy. Our legacy often mirrors the quality of our relationships—a web of interactions that ripple into the vast sea of lives we have touched.

On the other hand, our unfolding legacy influences our relational dynamics. Our actions, attitudes, and interactions, perceived as manifestations of our legacy, may propel others to reciprocate, nourish, sever, or redefine their bonds with us.

8.4. Conclusion: Forming the Human Dimension of Legacy

By carefully fostering relationships, we impart our legacy with a profound human dimension that transcends mere material possessions or accolades. This chapter has captured the essence of relationships in legacy building—exploring its importance, providing a step-by-step approach to fostering connections, and expounding the interactive relationship between legacy and our relational ties.

Success or wealth may be forgotten, but the relationships fostered and the impact made on people's lives echo into eternity. Define your legacy with love, empathy, and deep connections—ensuring the trace you leave behind is not merely a footmark in the sands of time, but a profound imprint on the human hearts that had the privilege of intersecting your life journey.

Chapter 9. Building Resilience: Navigating Through Storms

Resilience, often celebrated as the human spirit's ability to weather any storm no matter how ferocious, provides the groundwork for legacy-building. Encompassing both mental fortitude and emotional flexibility, resilience equips us to navigate obstacles, setbacks, or even failures that inevitably punctuate our journey towards a life of significance.

9.1. The Concept of Resilience

Resilience, from the Latin word 'resilio' meaning to rebound or recoil, essentially refers to the capacity to bounce back from challenging situations or adversities. It does not denote an absence of pain or feelings of distress but rather symbolizes the ability to continue functioning despite them. Life's inevitable tides of fortune, setbacks, and even tragedies don't discriminate. Yet, some people recover and even thrive in the face of adversity. The resounding trait that distinguishes these individuals can be encapsulated in one word- resilience.

In psychology, resilience is often described as a dynamic process or the resultant quality from a series of well-adjusted adaptive responses to trauma or adversity. It's not just about surviving after a storm but learning, growing, and possibly even flourishing because of it.

9.2. Importance of Building Resilience

Resilience-building is fundamental for navigating through life's storms, not just because it assists in recovery, but due to its potential for transformation. This transformative potential of resilience allows us to build stronger, more flexible 'selves' post-trauma. Resilience equips us with mental armor, allowing us to wade through difficulties, bouncing back stronger and more determined.

Moreover, resilience helps us redefine our relationship with adversity. Instead of perceiving adversities as insurmountable problems, resilience allows us to view these instances as stepping stones, rigorous tests of our strength, and integral parts of our journey toward building a meaningful legacy. Therefore, resilience forms the linchpin of our legacy-building efforts—a vital component that makes us stay committed to our course even when the going gets tough.

9.3. Strategies for Building Resilience

While resilience is partly the product of inherent personality traits, it's largely a learned behavior. Here are some strategies to help cultivate resilience:

- **Maintaining A Positive Outlook**: Positivity does not mean ignoring life's difficulties. It denotes acknowledging life's adversities while still fostering optimistic outlooks. Maintaining a hopeful outlook is a monumentally beneficial strategy, one that encourages resilience while promoting an overall sense of wellbeing.

- **Embracing Change**: Accepting and welcoming change is not only a hallmark of resilience but a necessity in a world constantly in flux. It involves viewing change not as a threat but as an opportunity for growth and learning.

- **Nurturing Relationships**: Ties to caring, supportive, and understanding people who validate our feelings and provide encouragement, significantly bolster resilience. Strengthening relationships and forging new, supportive friendships are integral to fostering resilience.

- **Taking Decisive Actions**: A problem-focused coping strategy is a key tenet of resilience. It involves dealing with problems head-on, taking decisive actions, and finding constructive solutions rather than resorting to avoidance or escapism.

- **Nurturing Self-Confidence**: A belief in oneself, one's abilities, and power is instrumental in fostering resilience. Self-efficacy buffers the impact of stress and promotes psychological well-being, thereby enhancing resilience.

- **Developing Coping Skills**: Learning and practicing stress-reduction techniques, such as mindfulness, meditation, and stress management, can significantly boost resilience. These skills assist in managing stress and circumventing potential psychological distress.

9.4. Resilience In The Face Of Failure

Every individual journey towards legacy building will inevitably encounter failure. It's important to understand that failure is not the opposite of success but an integral part of it. To build a long-lasting legacy, we must learn to withstand failures, absorb the learnings they provide, and forge ahead with renewed vigor. Resilience here acts as a vessel, sailing us through choppy waters until we reach our desired destination. Embracing failure, normalizing it, and learning from it will fortify our resilience and bring us one step closer to manifesting our desired legacy.

9.5. Conclusion: Resilience - The Legacy Builder's Armor

Resilience is no less than essential armor for anyone journeying towards creating a lasting and meaningful legacy. This mental and emotional shield enables us to withstand storms, transform defeats into victories and revisit adversities as opportunities. Empowering ourselves to understand, nurture and fortify our resilience might be one of the most rewarding tasks we undertake in our legacy-building efforts. At its core, resilience exists to remind us of our capacity to recover, learn, and continue striving for the realization of our purpose - the creation of our legacy - regardless of the intensity or duration of life's storms.

Chapter 10. Social Impact: Contributing to a Better World

Impactful journeys begin with meaningful first steps and there's no greater step towards a meaningful lifestyle than harnessing the power within to contribute to a better world. We find that the most effective means of contributing to the betterment of the world is through impactful social initiatives - actions driven towards positively influencing the societal, environmental and cultural aspects of our collective life.

10.1. Foundational Knowledge: What is Social Impact?

Human life is interwoven within a vast tapestry of social systems. These intricate connections shape our existence, influence our perception, and mold our progress. Actions affecting this social fabric, therefore, have the capacity to drive significant changes, and therein lays the essence of social impact - a term represented by the effects of actions that alter the life and condition of individuals, communities, and societies at large. Engaging in social impact activities allows us to put forth positive ripples that reach far beyond our immediate surroundings, contributing to change on a global scale.

Understanding this causality is fundamental to recognize that each one of us has the potential to generate social impact. We, as individuals, organizations or communities, can foster transformations across various segments of society; be it social, economic, or environmental.

10.2. Defining Your Contribution: Where to Start?

Before one embarks on the journey to impact civil society, it is important to define one's spheres of influence. These may be the spaces where your interest, passion, profession, or societal need intersects. Begin by identifying what social issues resonate with you - it could be child education, climate change, public health, or poverty alleviation. Next, assess your skills, expertise, and resources. How can they be utilized towards addressing those issues?

Assembling these variables may feel daunting, yet the process fosters clarity and presents a roadmap to your social impact journey. And remember, even small steps count. Initiative and persistence are key to driving change, and often, it is the cumulative effect of seemingly minor actions that precipitate substantial shifts in society.

10.3. Acting on Your Insights: Strategies for Impact

Once you've determined your pathway, there are several action strategies you can adopt.

Actively Volunteering: Donate your time and skills to organizations and causes aligned with your passions. Volunteer work is invaluable; it strengthens communities, resolves issues, and catalyzes positive change.

Donations and Sponsorships: If you are economically empowered, utilizing your wealth to support relevant causes or social startups can immensely augment your social footprint.

Responsive Consumption: Consuming responsibly by favoring ethical brands that promote fair trade, ecological sustainability, and social justice can possibly redirect global markets towards more sustainable practices.

Awareness Building: Share knowledge, information, and passionate accounts about the causes you support. The currents of informed dialogue can surge into waves of awareness, eventually culminating into a sea-change in public opinion and policies.

Policy Advocacy: Engage with policy-making processes to influence legislation and public policies aligned with the causes you champion.

10.4. Measuring Your Impact: The Feedback Loop

Understanding the difference you're making is integral to the process. Define metrics or indicators relevant to the actions taken and systematically measure your progress. Regular assessments provide a feedback loop for continuous enhancement of strategies while validating your commitment to the cause.

Remember, social impact is a journey of constant learning, adaptation, and growth. Every effort is significant, every action matters. Stay present, stay engaged, and keep pushing for the positive changes you wish to see. Your passion becomes your legacy - impacting the world in endearing ways, one step at a time.

Chapter 11. Reflection and Growth: The Continuous Journey

Life is not merely a sequence of random occurrences or a lineal stroll through time, rather it's an unending spiral of learning, reflecting upon our experiences, and refining our actions to develop deeper self-understanding and better alignment with our pursuits. Just as the tides of the sea perpetually advance, recede, and return anew, so too does the rhythm of reflection and growth that makes up the human journey. In this pivotal landscape filled with potential for growth, the onus is on you to engage in perennial self-improvement, understanding that the journey to leave a legacy, to have made a difference, is lifelong and calls for steady progress and frequent analysis.

11.1. The Reflective Process: Looking Inward To Move Forward

Understanding the value of reflection in our lives starts with seeing it not as an optional activity or a mere periodic task, but as an indispensable component of our evolution into becoming legacy builders. Reflection isn't simply reviewing actions and outcomes; it involves diving deep into the ocean of our thoughts, feelings, and experiences. Being able to recognize patterns in behaviours and identify areas of improvements helps in re-calibrating our compass and making necessary amendments. Remember that wisdom does not come from experiences alone, but from reflecting upon these experiences.

11.2. Biases and Blind Spots: Overcoming the Obstacles to Clear Vision

Although reflecting on our experiences is fruitful, biases and blind spots can distort our perception. A blind spot is an aspect of our character of which we're unaware, but can impact our decisions and actions. Often, such blind spots hamper your process of reflection, slowing your progress towards your legacy goals. By recognizing these unconscious patterns and biases, we can strive to overcome these limitations, unlocking our true self-awareness. Remember, a journey that starts with self-deception never leads to significant growth.

11.3. Lessons from Nature: The Cycle of Growth

Just as a mighty oak tree springs forth from a tiny acorn, we grow from the wealth of our experiences and reflections. In nature, we find perfect examples of consistent growth. Seasons change, and with them, so do the needs and behaviours of organisms. Just as these creatures adapt to the varying temperatures, food availabilities, and predatory threats, we too have to adapt to vacillating circumstances, constantly moulding our habits and characteristics to best fit our environment and goals. Developing adaptability and flexibleness not only aid our survival but also position us for thriving amidst uncertainty.

11.4. Gazing into the Future: Anticipating Changes and Continuing Growth

Learning from past experiences and using these lessons as a platform for future growth essential. Anticipating future challenges allows us to better prepare to confront them. Forward-thinking reflection is not about worrying or feeling anxious, but about learning from past patterns and predicting how current actions might impact the future. This process of forward reflection can be especially helpful in discerning which of our current habits will serve our legacy and which ones we might need to alter or eliminate.

11.5. The Power of Journaling: Reflection through Writing

One particularly effective tool to aid the reflection process is journaling. By committing our thoughts, feelings, and experiences to paper, we can gain perspective, notice trends and patterns, and meditate on our progress. This process elevifies personal growth and provides a record of our journey to be revisited in future reflection.

11.6. Foster a Growth Mindset: Embracing Challenges

Cultivating a growth mindset primes us to embrace challenges as stepping stones for development rather than seeing them as insurmountable hurdles. People with a growth mindset are aware that abilities and intelligence can be developed. By accepting failures and setbacks as part of the journey, you'll foster resilience and tenacity, key traits required to stay the course of building a significant legacy.

In conclusion, reflection and growth are undisputedly the continual processes on the path of legacy building. The cornerstone of leading a life of brilliant value lies not in the destination arrived at, but in the continuous journey of striving for excellence, accepting failures and learning, above all, evolving from each step taken. This chapter is an invitation for you to embrace the beautiful process of reflection and growth in your legacy-building journey. When approached with humility, patience, and openness, this is a journey that promises self-discovery, learning, and immense satisfaction.

www.ingramcontent.com/pod-product-compliance
Lightning Source LLC
Chambersburg PA
CBHW061545250726
48657CB00006B/2294